Jules J. Berman

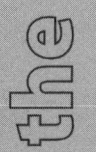the

RUBY
Programming Language

JONES AND BARTLETT PUBLISHERS
Sudbury, Massachusetts
BOSTON   TORONTO   LONDON   SINGAPORE

World Headquarters
Jones and Bartlett Publishers
40 Tall Pine Drive
Sudbury, MA 01776
978-443-5000
info@jbpub.com
www.jbpub.com

Jones and Bartlett Publishers Canada
6339 Ormindale Way
Mississauga, Ontario L5V 1J2
Canada

Jones and Bartlett Publishers International
Barb House, Barb Mews
London W6 7PA
United Kingdom

Jones and Bartlett's books and products are available through most bookstores and online book-sellers. To contact Jones and Bartlett Publishers directly, call 800-832-0034, fax 978-443-8000, or visit our website www.jbpub.com.

Substantial discounts on bulk quantities of Jones and Bartlett's publications are available to corporations, professional associations, and other qualified organizations. For details and specific discount information, contact the special sales department at Jones and Bartlett via the above contact information or send an email to specialsales@jbpub.com.

Production Credits
Acquisitions Editor: Tim Anderson
Production Director: Amy Rose
Editorial Assistant: Melissa Elmore
Senior Marketing Manager: Andrea DeFronzo
Manufacturing Buyer: Therese Connell
Composition: Northeast Compositors
Cover Design: Diana Coe
Cover Image: © IKO/ShutterStock, Inc.
Printing and Binding: Malloy, Inc.
Cover Printing: Malloy, Inc.

6048

Printed in the United States of America
12 11 10 09 08   10 9 8 7 6 5 4 3 2 1

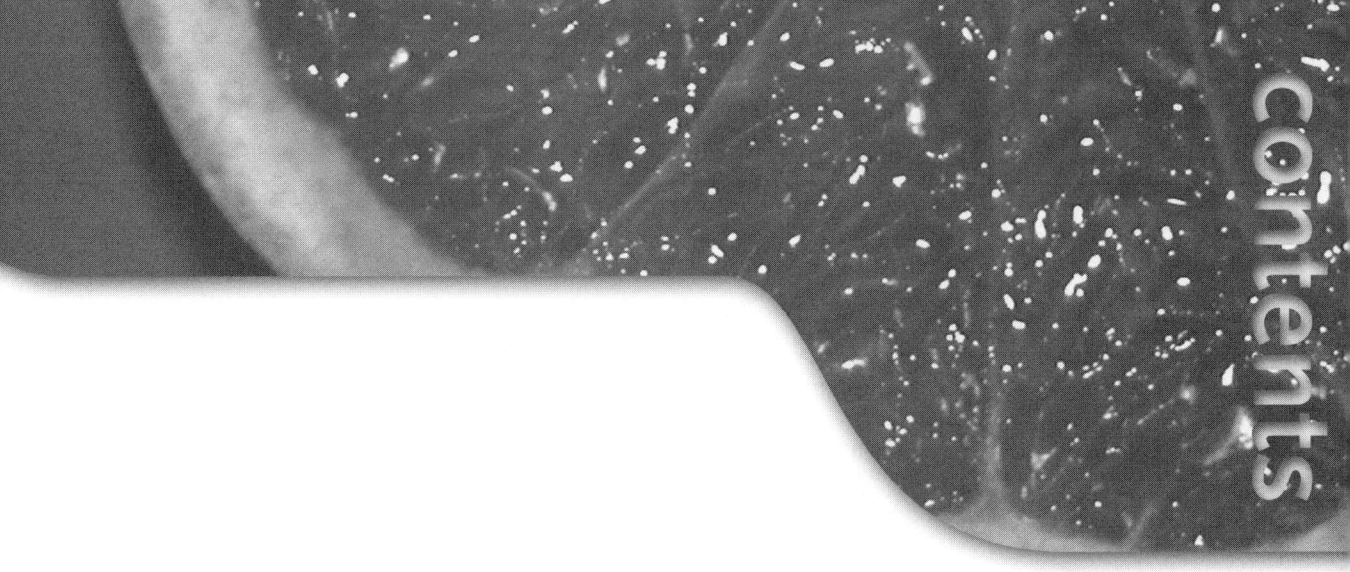

chapter 1

The Ruby Programming Language

After studying this material, you should be able to:

- Understand the basic features of object-oriented programming languages
- Understand class inheritance
- Describe the basic Ruby syntax used to send methods to objects
- Use `irb` (the interactive Ruby environment) to evaluate Ruby statements
- Understand the basic structure of a Ruby script
- Use some of the built-in Ruby classes (`String`, `IO`, `Numeric`, `Array`, `Hash`)
- Understand the difference between a class method and an instance method
- Create file objects and parse files line-by-line
- Use the Ruby Standard Library
- Import a RubyGem
- Write a Ruby script
- Create your own simple Ruby class and define an instance method for the class

1.1 Introduction to Ruby

What Is Ruby?

Ruby is an object-oriented programming language that was created in 1995 by Yukihiro Matsumoto (known as "Matz" to his devotees). Since then, Ruby has achieved enormous popularity both in its country of origin (Japan) and throughout the world. Class libraries built into the standard Ruby distribution provide the same functionality (usually with the same names) as the standard Perl modules and the standard Python library. As a consequence, both Perl programmers and Python programmers can easily migrate to Ruby.

Many programmers have found that Ruby lets them write well-designed object-oriented software applications in less time, with less code, and with less complexity than they could with any other programming language. In addition to the classes and modules packed in the standard Ruby distribution, Ruby programmers have access to Ruby libraries located throughout the world through RubyGem, a system for downloading and installing Ruby software located on remote servers.

To date, the most successful Ruby project has been Ruby on Rails, a framework for Web application development in Ruby. Ruby on Rails is, in large part, responsible for the rapidly growing popularity of the Ruby language.

Ruby is a scripting language, so you can write your Ruby programs as text files. These text files can then be launched from the command line of any operating system that has installed Ruby. Perl, Python, and Ruby are among the most popular scripting languages.

Readers who are interested in the scientific uses of Ruby might want to consider reading my book, *Ruby Programming for Medicine and Biology*, published by Jones and Bartlett Publishers in 2007.

Learning Ruby

Learning an object-oriented programming language, such as Ruby, is fundamentally different from learning an imperative programming language, such as C, Perl, or Basic. Ruby provides the programmer with five intellectual tools:

- A general syntax for the statements that will compose your Ruby programs.
- A set of familiar computational structures, such as `while` loops and `if` statements.
- A holder for your code. In the case of Ruby, it is the "script"—a simple text file that begins with a shebang line and ends with the word "exit" and that can be launched from a system command line.
- A library of built-in object methods.
- An object-oriented paradigm in which a desired script outcome is achieved through a succession of statements that send methods to objects.

A Ruby script has access to all of the classes and methods that are provided in the class libraries. Because the most common parts of a program are built into object-oriented languages, object-oriented programs tend to be much shorter than programs of equivalent functionality written in imperative programming languages. All of the programs provided here will involve less than a dozen lines of code.

You can achieve any of four levels of Ruby proficiency:

Level 1: Use the basic syntax of Ruby statements to create simple functional scripts. (Requires several hours of study.)

Level 2: Use the class and instance methods that are built into Ruby. (Requires several weeks of study.)

Level 3: Use the Ruby Standard Library and distributed RubyGems. (Requires several months of study.)

Level 4: Master the Ruby object-oriented paradigm to design your own class libraries and to develop full-scale, tested applications. (Requires several years of study.)

In this supplemental section, we will cover Level 1 and the most popular computational methods from Level 2.

Installing Ruby

Ruby is available for almost every popular operating system. Windows users can download a one-click installation package at

```
http://rubyinstaller.rubyforge.org/wiki/wiki.pl
```

or at

```
http://rubyforge.org/frs/?group_id=167
```

UNIX/Linux users can download Ruby at

```
http://www2.ruby-lang.org/en/20020102.html
```

The latest instructions for installing UNIX/Linux versions of Ruby are available from the distribution websites.

What Is a Ruby Statement?

The basic syntax of a Ruby statement is as follows:

```
<receiving object>.<sending method>(<arguments>){block}
```

In words, a method is sent to a receiving object, along with data included in a parenthesized argument or a code block. Let us look at a few examples of Ruby statements.

One of the built-in methods of the `String` class is `downcase`, which converts uppercase characters to their lowercase equivalents:

```
"Hello World".downcase
```

This statement yields

```
"hello world"
```

Another `String` method is `length`, which yields the number of characters in a String object:

```
"Hello World".length
```

This statement yields

```
11
```

Another `String` method is `split`, which breaks a string into parts and stores the parts in an `Array` object. An array is an ordered list.

```
"Hello World".split
```

This statement yields the `Array` object

```
["Hello", "World"]
```

The `split` method will split a string at a specified delimiter. When no delimiter is provided (as in our example), the `split` method will split on the space character.

In the next sections, you will learn how to use Ruby statements to perform computational tasks.

The Interactive Ruby Environment (`irb`)

Ruby comes with a convenient command-line environment, called `irb`, that permits you to evaluate single-line statements. Once Ruby is installed, you can invoke `irb` from the command line by typing `irb` and pressing the Enter key:

```
C:\>irb

irb(main):001:0>
```

As you can see, you get a new prompt. Ruby then waits while you type a statement. When you press the Enter key, Ruby evaluates the statement.

Like most other languages, Ruby can perform a variety of simple operations, using notations that are familiar to most programmers:

```
irb(main):001:0> 5 * 4 => 20
irb(main):002:0> [1,2,3,4] - [3,4] => [1, 2]
irb(main):003:0> "hello world".upcase => "HELLO WORLD"
irb(main):004:0> 5 == 3 => false
irb(main):005:0> 5 == 5 => true
irb(main):006:0> 5 > 3 => true
```

Notation

From this point forward, whenever we use the `irb` environment, we will shorten the ouput annotation to save space. For example,

```
irb(main):001:0>
```

will be abbreviated as

```
irb>
```

Method names and code will appear in `Courier font`. When we need to specify an instance method name along with its class, we will use a parenthesized concatenation in the form (`Class#method`).

Although line comments are not used in these materials, Ruby code comments are marked by a # (pound) sign. The Ruby interpreter ignores line text occurring after a #.

1.2 Object–Oriented Programming

Creating Ruby Objects

The power of an object-oriented language becomes evident when you start creating your own objects and sending those objects class-appropriate methods.

In Ruby, all character strings are objects of class `String`. We can create a new instance object of class `String` by sending the `new` method to class `String`. The contents of the instance object will be a string that we supply as an argument to the `new` method:

```
irb> my_string = String.new("Hello World") => "Hello World"
```

The `irb` environment evaluates the statement `String.new("Hello World")` and yields the string `"Hello World"`.

That was easy, but it may not seem as if we have accomplished very much. In reality, we have accomplished a great deal: We have created a new instance object that inherits all of the methods from class `String`.

Ruby knows the class of every object. The `class` method, when sent to an object, yields the class of the object. As an example, let us ask Ruby to tell us the class of our newly created `my_string` object:

```
irb> my_string.class => String
```

Yes, the object `my_string` is an instance of class `String`. Now we decide to discover all of the methods that are available to the `my_string` object by sending the `methods` method to `my_string`:

```
irb> my_string.methods =>
["methods", "instance_eval", "%", "rindex", "map", "<<", "split", "any?", "dup",
"sort", "strip", "size", "instance_variables", "downcase", "min", "gsub!",
"count", "include?", "succ!", "instance_of?", "extend", "downcase!", "intern",
"squeeze!", "eql?", "*", "next", "find_all", "each", "rstrip!", "each_line",
"+","id", "sub", "slice!", "hash", "singleton_methods", "tr", "replace",
"inject", "reverse", "taint", "sort_by", "lstrip", "frozen?",
"instance_variable_get", "capitalize", "max", "chop!", "kind_of?", "capitalize!",
"scan", "select", "to_a", "each_byte", "type", "casecmp", "gsub",
"protected_methods", "empty?", "to_str","partition", "tr_s", "tr!", "match",
"grep", "rstrip", "to_sym", "instance_variable_set", "next!", "swapcase",
"chomp!", "method", "is_a?", "swapcase!", "ljust", "respond_to?", "between?",
"reject", "to_s", "upto", "hex", "sum", "class", "require_gem", "reverse!",
"chop", "<=>", "insert", "<", "tainted?", "private_methods", "==", "delete",
"dump", "===", "__id__", "member?", "tr_s!", "unpack", ">", "concat", "nil?",
"untaint", "succ", "find", "strip!", "each_with_index", ">=", "gem", "to_i",
"rjust", "<=", "send", "display", "index", "collect", "inspect", "slice", "oct",
"all?", "clone", "object_id", "length", "entries", "chomp", "=~", "require",
"public_methods", "upcase", "sub!", "squeeze", "__send__", "upcase!", "crypt",
"delete!", "equal?", "freeze", "detect", "zip", "[]", "lstrip!", "center", "[]=",
"to_f"]
```

Wow! Our new object has dozens of methods available to it. In Ruby, every instance object can use any of the instance methods included in its class as well as every instance method included in every one of its ancestor classes. This ability, which is called inheritance, is one of the most important features in every object-oriented language.

Just for fun, let us select one of the methods from the list, `reverse!`, and send it to the `my_string` object:

```
irb> my_string.reverse!  => "dlroW olleH"
```

We then reverse this operation to get our original string:

```
irb> my_string.reverse! => "Hello World"
```

Let us try the `chop` method and see what it does to `my_string`:

```
irb> my_string.chop => "Hello Worl"
```

As we see, this method chopped the last character from `my_string`. Let us evaluate the contents of `my_string` after the last character has been chopped:

```
irb> my_string => "Hello World"
```

What happened? Why has the "d" been restored to the end of `my_string`? In Ruby, methods are usually nondestructive. In other words, when a method is sent to the object, it does not change the contents of the object. Although the `chop` method yielded a truncated string (which we could have then assigned to another object), it did not change the original `my_string` object.

Sometimes we may prefer to use a destructive method, which changes the contents of the object receiving the method. Ruby provides destructive equivalents of many built-in methods; they are usually identifiable by the exclamation point at the end of the method. For example, Ruby has both a `chop` method and a `chop!` method. Let us send the `chop!` method to the `my_string` object:

```
irb> my_string.chop! => "Hello Worl"
```

Now let us look at the contents of the `my_string` object:

```
irb> my_string => "Hello Worl"
```

In this case, `chop!` has changed the data contained in the `my_string` object.

Ruby Inheritance

In the prior section, we created the object `my_string` as an instance of class `String`. Ruby provides a method called `superclass` that returns a class's direct ancestor. Let us ask Ruby for the class above class `String` by sending the `superclass` method to `String`:

```
irb> String.superclass => Object
```

The `superclass` method is a method of class `Class` and can be sent to any class. It is an example of reflection (sometimes called introspection); reflection methods tell us something about the role or the properties of a Ruby object.

Ruby has dozens of built-in classes. The classes that programmers use most often include the following:

```
String
Array
Numeric
Hash
IO
```

Class IO has the important subclass File. Figure 1 shows class Numeric in schematic form.

In an object-oriented language, classes inherit methods from their ancestral classes. When the name of a method is sent to an object in a Ruby statement, Ruby looks within the class of the object for the corresponding method. If it finds the method in the current class, it executes the method for the receiving object. If it fails to find the method in the current class, it looks in the next-higher class for the named method. It continues in this way until it finds the named method or it exhausts the hierarchy. If the hierarchy is exhausted without finding the named method, Ruby sends an error message.

As an example, let us create a new instance object of class Array and send it the method (which we have already demonstrated) named chop:

```
irb> my_array = Array.new([1,2,"ice cream",4]) => [1, 2, "ice cream", 4]
irb> my_array.chop
NoMethodError: private method 'chop' called for [1, 2, "ice cream", 4]:Array
        from (irb):13
```

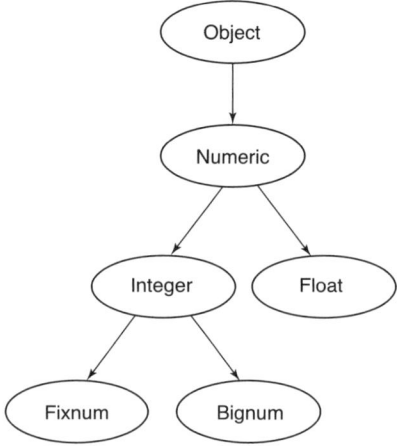

Figure 1   *Ruby class hierarchy for number-related classes. Class* Numeric *is a subclass of class* Object. Numeric *has two subclasses,* Integer *and* Float. Integer *has two subclasses,* Fixnum *and* Bignum.

When we sent `my_array` the `chop` method, we got an error message; because `chop` is a Ruby method for class `String`, rather than class `Array`. Furthermore, class `String` is not an ancestor of class `Array`, so methods in class `String` are unavailable to instance objects of class `Array`. In addition, none of the ancestors of class `Array` happen to have a method of their own that is named `chop`.

Now let us send the `superclass` method to the `Object` class to determine the next-higher class:

```
irb> Object.superclass => nil
```

Ruby returns `nil` because there is no class higher than class `Object`. The `nil` object is one of the most fascinating and powerful concepts in Ruby, and it is one of the features that distinguishes Ruby from languages that use a Boolean true/false to evaluate the success of operations. For example, in Perl, everything is true or false. If an operation fails, Perl usually assigns the value `False` to the result. Ruby yields `nil`—the nothing object—to unsuccessful operations. The `nil` object provides Ruby with the ability to avoid incorrect logical inferences and greatly enhances the value of Ruby as a language that supports logical operations.

Class Methods and Instance Methods

In Ruby, methods in a class are either class methods or instance methods. An instance method can be sent to any instance of a class for which the method is defined; it can also be sent to any instance of any subclass of the class. A class method can be sent to the class in which it is defined and to any subclass of that class. An instance method cannot be sent to a class object, and a class method cannot be sent to an instance object.

So, when do you use an instance method and when do you use a class method? In general, class methods create or initialize conditions for newly created instance objects, or they set or obtain information pertaining to the operating system or the Ruby environment. Instance methods are the various class-specific operations that typically add data to instance objects, modify instance objects, or evaluate instance objects. In the built-in Ruby classes, the instance methods handily outnumber the class methods.

The most commonly used `Class` method is `new`. In a Ruby script, new instance objects are created with the `new` method specific for the class to which the instance object will belong. We have already used the `new` method to create instances of the `String` and `Array` classes.

Method Polymorphism

In Ruby, different methods in different classes may have the same name. In fact, it is common programming practice to include methods in a subclass that override methods of the same name in a superclass (ancestor class). Polymorphism is the property wherein a software object behaves differently under different conditions.

There are many ways of achieving polymorphism. For example, method polymorphism can often be achieved by providing class methods that share a name with methods included in other classes. In this case, the behavior of a named method will vary from object to object depending on the class to which the object belongs. In Ruby, when you want to discuss a particular method, you need to specify which class contains the method. The standard shorthand for conveying the name of a method in descriptive text is to write the class name followed by a pound sign followed by the method name:

> Array#length (the class `Array length` method)
>
> Hash#length (the class `Hash length` method)
>
> String#length (the class `String length` method)

In Ruby, every class is related to every other class in the sense that all classes descend from class `Object`. Stretching the point, the same principle applies to all terrestrial organisms: That is, we all descend from a common primordial organism. In practical terms, two classes are related if one class is an ancestor of the other class. Two classes are unrelated if neither class is an ancestor of the other.

General Rules of Inheritance in Ruby

1. Ruby has a hierarchy of classes and subclasses. The highest class is `Object`. Every object in Ruby is a descendant of class `Object`.

2. Classes contain class methods and instance methods. Class methods can be sent only to a class. Instance methods can be sent only to an instance object of a class. The class methods are often used to provide system information or to create new instance objects. The instance methods are the functions and complex operations that are sent, along with data arguments, to instance objects, and that produce the desired output of a script.

3. The primary purpose of a class is to create instance objects that use the instance methods included in the class. The creation of instance objects is usually achieved by sending the `new` method to the class and providing a name for the newly created instance object.

4. Every class has only one direct ancestor (also known as the superclass). A class can have any number of subclasses.

5. Every instance object in Ruby inherits the instance methods of its current class as well as the methods of its ancestor (lineage) classes. Because every object in Ruby is a descendant of class `Object`, every Ruby object inherits all of the methods of class `Object`.

6. A method of a given name may occur in several different and unrelated classes. For example, several unrelated classes have their own `each` instance method, and most classes have their own `new` class method. This duplication of method names poses no problem in Ruby, because an object will only respond to the method that is appropriate for its own class.

7. A method of a given name may occur in several related classes. For example, a class may have a `new` class method, and its superclass may also have a new class method, and so on. In Ruby, this duplication poses no conflict. A class or a class instance object will receive the method of its own class, if the named method is present in the class. If the method is not present, Ruby will try to find the method in the next-higher class, and so on, until the class hierarchy is exhausted.

1.3   Writing and Executing a Short Ruby Script

Getting User Input

Ruby has two ways to execute code: through the `irb` environment or through Ruby scripts. Ruby scripts are text files that can be constructed in any text editor, such as Notepad. Word processors that insert special formatting notation into document files cannot be used to create Ruby scripts. Always provide your script files with the `.rb` suffix.

Your first Ruby script, `getinput.rb`, will retrieve a line of keyboarded input and redisplay it on your computer monitor:

```
#!/usr/bin/ruby
puts "Enter anything and press the Enter key"
input = STDIN.gets.chomp!
puts "You just entered \"#{input}\""
exit
```

To launch a Ruby script, invoke the script name from your operating system's prompt line (the `C:\>` prompt for Windows users):

```
C:\>ruby getinput.rb
```

A line of text appears on your computer screen:

```
Enter anything and press the Enter key
```

You enter some text ("hello world" in this example) and press the Enter key. Ruby collects your input and returns it as a quotation within a sentence:

```
You just entered "hello world"
```

Let us review each line of the `getinput.rb` script. The first line is as follows:

```
#!/usr/local/bin/ruby
```

This line tells the Ruby interpreter that the file is a Ruby script. The first two characters are always `#!`, the so-called shebang. The shebang gets its name from the pound sign (recognized by musicians as the sharp sign) followed by the exclamation point (the bang). By tradition, the shebang is the first two characters of every script in every scripting language (Perl, Python, Ruby, Awk). Following the shebang is the path to the Ruby interpreter. For Windows users, the shebang line has no meaning. The path to Ruby is automatically registered into the Windows operating system during Ruby installation. For some UNIX/Linux users, this path statement should be written to contain their system path to the Ruby interpreter. The next line is

```
puts "Enter anything and press the Enter key"
```

This line uses the `puts` method, which sends a string to an IO object (input/output object). The default destination of a `puts` method is standard output (`STDOUT`, your monitor).

```
input = STDIN.gets.chomp!
```

This line tells Ruby to wait until you enter a line of text. The `gets` method is sent to `STDIN` (standard input—in this case, your keyboard) and retrieves your input text. The `chomp!` method removes the last character from the input text (the newline character generated when you pressed the Enter key), and the resulting `String` object is provided with the name `input`. In Ruby, methods sent to an object, such as `get` and `chomp!`, can be chained together, saving many lines of code.

```
puts "You just entered \"#{input}\""
```

The `"#{object}"` notation is Ruby's way of retrieving the string assigned to the object. In this case, we use `"#{input}"` to extract the string contents from the `input` object. A slash escape character, `"\"`, is placed before each quotation mark to indicate that the character that follows (the quotation mark) is to be treated as a regular character and not as a special Ruby character indicating the end of a string expression.

Using Conditional Structures

Ruby has the common `while`, `for`, `if`, and `unless` structures. For example, here is the `did.rb` script.

```
#!/usr/local/bin/ruby
my_value = 5
your_value = 0
while your_value < my_value
    your_value = your_value + 1
    puts your_value
end
exit
```

By this time, the Ruby code should be self-explanatory. The output is shown here:

```
c:\>ruby did.rb
1
2
3
4
5
```

Class Range

Class `Range` represents intervals. This class has an `each` method that iterates over the members of the range—that is, over the included elements. The `Range` syntax is `(first..last)` to indicate all values between and including the first and last values and `(first...last)` to indicate all values between and including the first value but excluding the last value. For example,

```
irb>(1..5).each{|x|puts x}
1
2
3
4
5
```

Using Block Structures

Our second Ruby script, `interest.rb`, computes six generations of accrued growth from an initial quantity of 1000 (dollars), increasing at 5 percent per unit time (years):

```
#!/usr/local/bin/ruby
principal = 1000
(1..6).each do
  |x|
  principal = principal*(1.05)
  print(x, " ", principal, "\n")
  end
exit
```

The output is shown here:

```
c:\>ruby interest.rb
1 1050.0
2 1102.5
3 1157.625
4 1215.50625
5 1276.2815625
6 1340.095640625
```

Let us review the interest.rb script.

```
principal = 1000
```

Here we assign the number 1000 to principal. In Ruby, everything is an object. Thus, unlike in other languages, principal is not a variable whose value is 1000; principal is an object that can be assigned a number to which it refers. This subtle difference has many consequences in an object-oriented language. The most important difference is that, as an object, principal has access to object methods appropriate for its class. If principal were just another way of saying "1000," it would have no facility to receive methods designed for its class.

Let us look at the next five lines as a group:

```
(1..6).each do
  |x|
  principal = principal*(1.05)
  print(x, " ", principal, "\n")
end
```

The first line is an iterator for a block of code, where (1..6) specifies a range of numbers from 1 to 6. The each method iterates over the elements of the Range object, passing each element to the block. Each element is assigned to the object surrounded by straight brackets (|x|) with each loop of the block. The statements of the block are executed in each loop.

```
principal = principal*(1.05)
```

The asterisk is the multiplication operator in Ruby. The value assigned to the principal object is recalculated and reassigned with each loop.

```
print(x, " ", principal, "\n")
```

The `print` method sends a string to standard output (STDOUT, the computer monitor). This string consists of the character values of the concatenated objects within the parentheses. We will be seeing a lot of the \n character, which scripting languages interpret as the newline character.

The end of the code block is signified by the word `"end"`.

Chaining Ruby Methods in a Single Ruby Statement

The `combo.rb` script takes a string of words and produces every ordered fragment of words from the string. For instance, "I am here" would yield:

```
I
am
here
I am
am here
I am here
```

The `combo.rb` script is shown here:

```
#!/usr/bin/ruby
sentence = "Ruby is the best language"
cum_array = Array.new
sentence_array = sentence.split
length = sentence_array.size
length.times do
   (1..sentence_array.size).each do
     |place_length|
     cum_array << sentence_array.slice(0,place_length).join(" ")
   end
   sentence_array.shift
end
print cum_array.join("\n")
exit
```

The output of `combo.rb` is shown here:

```
C:\>ruby combo.rb
Ruby
Ruby is
Ruby is the
Ruby is the best
Ruby is the best language
is
is the
```

```
is the best
is the best language
the
the best
the best language
best
best language
language
```

Let us review this script line by line.

```
#!/usr/bin/ruby
sentence = "Ruby is the best language"
sentence_array = sentence.split
length = sentence_array.size
```

We begin with a sentence, which we transform into an array with the split method. Class String's split method is used in virtually every script that parses strings of words. The split method breaks a string at locations that match a regular expression and returns an array containing the pieces of the string. If no regular expression is provided, split breaks the sentence at the space character.

We need to know the number of words in the array, which is accomplished by using class Array's size method:

```
length = sentence_array.size
```

The next lines of the script describe an iteration block within an iteration block:

```
length.times do
(1..sentence_array.size).each do
  |place_length|
  puts sentence_array.slice(0,place_length).join(" ")
end
sentence_array.shift
end
```

This short snippet of code does the bulk of the work of the script. The outer block has this form:

```
length.times do
  .
  .
  .
end
```

The block tells Ruby to iterate over the code between the `do...end` for a number of times determined by the value of `length`. In this case, `length` is the number of words in the phrase "Ruby is the best language"–that is, 5.

Nested inside the block is another block:

```
(1..sentence_array.size).each do
|place_length|]
puts sentence_array.slice(0,place_length).join(" ")
end
```

This inside block has the following form:

```
(1..n).each do
| . |
.
end
```

This block will iterate in a range from `1` to `n`. The `each` method applied to a range assigns each iterated number from the range to a variable specified between the vertical bars.

```
(1..sentence_array.size).each do
|place_length|
```

In this case, every loop of the inside block will iterate over a range that extends to the size of the array `sentence_array` and passes the range value for each iteration to `place_length`. At each iteration, the `slice` method is sent to `sentence_array`. The `slice` method cuts out an array from `sentence_array`, consisting of the array elements specified by the parenthesized arguments. In this case, the arguments to `slice` are `0` and `place_length`. Thus the slice of `sentence_array` will consist of the elements from element zero (the first element) to element `place_length` (the range number passed by the each method in the current loop). The `join(" ")` method sent to the result of the `sentence_array.slice(0,place_length)` statement transforms the sliced array to a string in which each element from the array joined by a space. Finally, the `puts` method sends the resulting string to the monitor:

```
puts sentence_array.slice(0,place_length).join(" ")
```

The inside iteration loop is followed by another Ruby statement:

```
sentence_array.shift
```

After each iteration of the inner loop, the `sentence_array` instance object is sent the `shift` method. The `shift` method removes the first element from the array and returns an array that is shorter (by one element) than the original array. Thus, after each range of iterations of the inner loop, `sentence_array` will be reduced in length by one element and returned for another turn of the outer loop.

What does the nested loop accomplish? The nested loop takes a string of words and produces a slice that consists of the first word, then the first word plus the second word, then the first word plus the second word plus the third word, and so forth, until the full list of words is produced. Then the loop knocks off the first word and repeats the process, producing the second word, then the second word plus the third word, and so forth. The output from each iteration continues through the nested iterators.

Nested iterations are incredibly powerful tools that are much less complex than their written explanation would suggest. After you start writing your own programs, you will find it very easy to write nested iterators.

Ruby supports two equivalent syntactic representations of iteration blocks. In our example script, we used the following syntax:

```
object.method(arguments) do
|iteration_variable|
code lines
end
```

An equivalent syntax is:

```
object.method(arguments){|iteration_variable| code}
```

The first syntax is preferred if the code contains multiple lines.

In Ruby, multiple statements can appear on a single line (or in a single lined block) by placing a semicolon between each statement:

```
object.method(arguments){|iteration_variable|statement1;
statement2}
```

Class `Hash`

A hash is an unordered list of key/value pairs. "Associative array" and "dictionary" are both synonyms for "hash." In Ruby, hash objects are instances of class `Hash` and have a variety of powerful methods at their disposal. We use hashes in most of the Ruby scripts provided here. We can create key/value hash elements as shown in the `hash.rb` script:

```
#!/usr/local/bin/ruby
my_hash = Hash.new
my_hash["C0000005"] = "(131)I-Macroaggregated Albumin"
my_hash["C0000039"] = "1,2-Dipalmitoylphosphatidylcholine"
my_hash["C0000052"] = "1,4-Alpha-Glucan Branching Enzyme"
my_hash["C0000074"] = "1-Alkyl-2-Acylphosphatidates"
my_hash["C0000084"] = "1-Carboxyglutamic Acid"
my_hash.each {|key,value| STDOUT.print(key, " --- ", value,
"\n")}
exit
```

In the statement that follows, "C0000005" is the key and "(131)I-Macroaggregated Albumin" is the hash value. Together they constitute a key/value hash element:

```
my_hash["C0000005"] = "(131)I-Macroaggregated Albumin"
```

The last line of the Ruby script uses the Hash#each method. The each method iteratively submits hash elements (that is, key/value pairs) to a block of code. The code block prints to the monitor each key and value for each iteration, including a " --- " string between the two variables and ending each string with a newline character.

```
my_hash.each {|key,value| STDOUT.print(key, " --- ",
value,"\n")}
```

The output is shown here:

```
C:\>ruby hash.rb
C0000005 --- (131)I-Macroaggregated Albumin
C0000039 --- 1,2-Dipalmitoylphosphatidylcholine
C0000084 --- 1-Carboxyglutamic Acid
C0000074 --- 1-Alkyl-2-Acylphosphatidates
C0000052 --- 1,4-alpha-Glucan Branching Enzyme
```

Notice that the output order of the key/value pairs does not correspond to the order in which the hash elements were created in the hash.rb script. Recall that a hash is an *unordered* collection of key/value pairs. Ruby stores the hash values internally to facilitate retrieval of pairs based on a lookup indexed to the key. Although the internal order makes sense to Ruby, the printed output of key/value pairs appears random to humans.

When should you use hashes? Hashes have particular utility when you have lists of data elements, each of which is intimately bound to another element. For instance, in a biomedical nomenclature, a term might be bound to a code number (which uniquely identifies the term) or to a definition (which explains the term) or to a byte location (which tells you the precise spot in the nomenclature that holds the term) or to a specific website (where the term is used). In all of these cases, there is a term, and there is a value associated with the term.

An advantage of hash data structures relates to the speed with which Ruby can access key/value pairs. When you provide Ruby with the key for any key/value pair, Ruby can quickly access the associated value. It accomplishes this task without actually traversing all of the key/value pairs in the hash, because its internal structure for key/value pairs supports quick access.

Zipf Distribution

Computational linguists rely on Zipf distributions to identify the frequency of occurrence of objects in a collection of objects. The zipf.rb script produces an alphabetized list of the words in a string, with the number of occurrences following each word.

```
#!/usr/local/bin/ruby
freq = Hash.new(0)
my_string = "A man, a plan, a canal, Panama"
my_string.downcase.scan(/\w+/){|word| freq[word] =
freq[word]+1}
freq.keys.sort.each {|k| print k, " - ", freq[k], "\n"}
exit
```

The ouput of zipf.rb is shown here:

```
C:\>ruby zipf.rb
a - 3
canal - 1
man - 1
panama - 1
plan - 1
```

Let us review the zipf.rb script line by line. First, we declare a new Hash object and a string to be parsed:

```
freq = Hash.new(0)
my_string = "A man, a plan, a canal, Panama"
```

The Zipf distribution of the words in the sentence is created in a single line of Ruby code:

```
my_string.downcase.scan(/\w+/){|word|freq[word] =
freq[word]+1}
```

The string is converted to lowercase and then parsed by the `scan` iteration method. The `scan` method matches a pattern against a string and pushes each matching substring into an array or passes each matching substring to a block. In this case, we provide the scan method with a block so that the latter behavior is followed. The matching pattern is /\w+/, where the \w character represents alphanumerics (0–9 plus any alphabetic character) and the underscore. Words are essentially concatenations of alphanumerics bordered by non-alphanumerics, such as a space, a period, or a newline character. In our example, each matching word is passed to the block, where it is added as a key to the `freq Hash` object. Each time the same key occurs in the block, the value associated with key is incremented by one.

```
freq[word] = freq[word]+1
```

The initial value associated with each key is zero. The next line of Ruby code takes the `freq Hash` object, produces an array from the keys (with the `keys` method), sorts the keys alphabetically, and, for each element in the array, prints to the monitor the element and the element's value.

```
freq.keys.sort.each {|k| print k, " - ", freq[k], "\n"}
```

A Concordance

Let us create an object of class `File` and use some of the techniques we have learned to create a file concordance. A concordance is an index that includes every location of every word in a file. We will use a file composed of the first 10 lines of Hamlet's soliloquy:

"To be, or not to be—that is the question:

Whether 'tis nobler in the mind to suffer

The slings and arrows of outrageous fortune

Or to take arms against a sea of troubles

And by opposing end them. To die, to sleep—

No more—and by a sleep to say we end

The heartache, and the thousand natural shocks

That flesh is heir to. 'Tis a consummation

Devoutly to be wished. To die, to sleep—

To sleep—perchance to dream: ay, there's the rub,"

This text is put into the file `hamlet.txt`.

We will use 12 lines of Ruby code in `concord.rb` to prepare a complete concordance:

```
#!/usr/local/bin/ruby
f = File.open("hamlet.txt")
```

```
place = Hash.new(""); wordarray = Array.new
f.each do
   |line|
   line.downcase!
   line.gsub!(/[^a-z ]/," ")
   wordarray = line.split.uniq
   next if wordarray == []
   wordarray.each{|word| place[word] = "#{place[word]}
#{f.lineno}"}
   wordarray = []
end
place.keys.sort.each{|key| puts "#{key} #{place[key]}"}
exit
```

Here is the partial output, consisting of the first 20 lines of alphabetized words and their line locations:

```
C:\>ruby concord.rb
a   4  6  8
against  4
and   3  5  6  7
arms   4
arrows   3
ay   10
be   1  9
by   5  6
consummation   8
devoutly   9
die   5  9
dream   10
end   5  6
flesh   8
fortune   3
heartache   7
heir   8
in   2
is   1  8
mind   2
```

The `concord.rb` script creates a concordance for a text file. Each word in the concordance file is followed by the list of lines from the text in which the word appears. In this case, we chose `hamlet.txt` as our text file. If you wish, you can verify the output by comparing the line occurrences in the Hamlet soliloquy against each word in the concordance.

How did Ruby do it? The `concord.rb` script parses each line of text and creates an array of the words from the line of text.

By now, most of the statements in the script should be familiar to you. One statement that might seem strange to nonprogrammers is this one:

```
line.gsub!(/[^a-z ]/," ")
```

This statement tells Ruby to substitute a space at every location in the line where a character is encountered that is neither a letter of the alphabet nor a space character. How can Ruby understand this complex instruction with such a short line of code? It is all done with Regex (regular expressions), a formal syntax for describing string patterns. This syntax, once mastered, permits programmers to write remarkably clever and useful pattern-matching routines. Many different programming languages and markup languages use the same Regex syntax (including Perl, Python, and XML).

An example of Regex is `"b[na]+"`, which represents a string pattern that begins with the letter "b" and is followed by any one of the letters "n" or "a," with at least one occurrence. Thus "banana" would match the regular expression, as would "baaaaaa," signifying that the regular expression could be useful to computer programmers, monkeys, or sheep.

In the example from our Ruby script, the Regex pattern is `/[^a-z ]/`, which matches an occurrence of characters that are neither "a" through "z" nor a space character. The ^ character within a Regex expression block (`[]`) indicates the negation. The `gsub!` method is the destructive repeat-substitution method that will operate on every occurrence of a pattern within an object, substituting matched patterns with the provided alternative—a space (`" "`) in this case.

Regex is heady stuff for programmers who are new to the notation. Nevertheless, mastering Regex is well worth the effort.

Returning to the example, the line is split at the space character and the returned array is cleared of repeat items (using the `uniq` method). The resulting array of items is assigned to the `wordarray` instance object:

```
wordarray = line.split.uniq
```

For each word in `wordarray`, a key/value pair is created. The key is the word itself. The value is the line number in which the word appears (determined with class `IO`'s `lineno` method) concatenated to the prior value associated with the key. This scheme effectively builds a list of line numbers on which the key occurs. The key/value pair is assigned to the `place` Hash instance object:

```
wordarray.each{|word| place[word] = "#{place[word]}
#{f.lineno}"}
```

At the end of each line iteration through the file, the `wordarray` instance object is emptied in preparation for receiving the words on the next line. The keys in the `place Hash` instance object are extracted as an array using the `keys` method and are subsequently sorted before the next iteration with `each`. Every iteration through the sorted array of keys prints the key, followed by its value.

```
place.keys.sort.each{|key| puts "#{key} #{place[key]}"}
```

Remember, the "`#{object}`" notation is Ruby's way of retrieving the string assigned to the object.

1.4 Advanced Features of Ruby

Creating a Ruby Class

It may seem odd to include creating a Ruby class in this section covering advanced Ruby features. Creating new classes is one of the defining properties of all object-oriented programming languages. Most Ruby programming, however, is done with Ruby's built-in classes and methods. Indeed, Ruby is so self-sufficient that beginning programmers do not need to create their own classes. When you want to create a class, you will find it a very simple process.

In this section, we will create a class and provide the class with a class method. Inside a class, class methods are defined differently from instance methods. Here is an example where we create a class (`Person`) and a class method (`name`):

```
#!/usr/local/bin/ruby
class Person
    def Person.name
        return "Jules"
    end
end
puts Person.name
exit
```

A class method definition starts with `def` followed by the name of the class followed by a dot followed by the class method name (which happens to be `name` in this example). After the classs is defined, the class method can be sent directly to the class: `puts Person.name`.

Now, let us modify the same script, this time creating an instance method that has the same functionality as the class method:

```
#!/usr/local/bin/ruby
class Person
    def name
        return "Jules"
    end
```

```
end
me = Person.new
puts me.name
exit
```

Here the name of the method is not preceded by the name of the class. In Ruby, this is the difference between creating a class method and an instance method. Once the class is defined, the instance method can be used by creating a new instance of the class and sending the instance method to the instance object: `puts me.name`.

Let us modify the script once again, this time assigning a superclass to class `Person`:

```
#!/usr/local/bin/ruby
class Person < String
    def name
        return "Jules"
    end
end
me = Person.new
puts me.name
exit
```

By adding `< String` to the top line of the class definition, we make `Person` a subclass of class `String`. Class `Person` will inherit all of the methods of class `String` and all of the methods of the ancestors of class `String`.

In just a few lines of code, we have demonstrated the basics of class creation, method creation, and inheritance!

Using the Ruby Standard Library

Standard Libraries are bundled in Ruby distributions. They are different from built-in classes, but just as easy to use. As an example, let us work with the Ruby Standard Library, Base64.

Although we distinguish text files from binary files, all files are actually binary files. Sequential bytes of 8 bits are converted to ASCII equivalents, and if the ASCII equivalents are alphanumerics, we call the result a text file. If the ASCII values of 8-bit sequential file chunks are non-alphanumeric, we call the result a binary file. Actually, any file can be converted into something akin to a text file by dividing the file into 6-bit chunks and assigning each 6-bit chunk an alphanumeric ASCII character with two leading zeros (that is, a 0-padded 6-bit ASCII value, which is equivalent to a Base64 character). Binary can be inter-converted with Base64. In fact, Base64 conversion is sometimes used to represent a binary file as an alphanumeric file. Alphanumeric files are useful because they can be ported inside formats that require plain ASCII text (such as HTML and XML). It is easy to convert a text string into Base64 and to covert the Base64 representation back into ordinary text.

Let us use the Base64 Standard Library in the `base64.rb` script:

```
#!/usr/local/bin/ruby
require 'base64'
text = "The secret of life"
encoded = Base64.encode64(text)
puts("This is the encoded text ... #{encoded}")
decoded = Base64.decode64(encoded)
puts("This is the decoded text ... #{decoded}")
exit
```

The output of the script is shown here:

```
C:\>ruby base64.rb
This is the encoded text ... VGhlIHNlY3JldCBvZiBsaWZl
This is the decoded text ... The secret of life
```

The Base64 Standard Library is imported into the `base64.rb` script by using the `require` method:

```
require 'base64'
```

This process is sometimes referred to as "requiring" a library into a script. Once done, the methods of the required library are available to the script.

```
encoded = Base64.encode64(text)
```

The `encode` method, when sent to the Base64 class along with a sample of text as the method parameter, creates a new instance object.

A modified script can encode (and then decode) an entire file into Base64:

```
#!/usr/local/bin/ruby
require 'base64'
image_file = File.open("walnut.jpg").binmode
image_file_string = image_file.read
b64 = Base64.encode64(image_file_string)
puts b64.slice(0,300)
regular = Base64.decode64(b64)
out_file = File.open("walnew.jpg", "w").binmode
out_file.write(regular)
exit
```

In this script, we convert the binary image file `walnut.jpg`, to Base64. We send the file the `binmode` method, which tells Ruby to treat the file as a binary file and to ignore characters contained in the file that have special meanings (such as line breaks and end-of-file characters).

Extending Ruby

You can extend the functionality of Ruby by taking advantage of freely available applications that can be downloaded from the Internet. Two extensions that can be used together to display and manipulate images are Tk, a graphical user interface (GUI) application, and ImageMagick. Tk employs widgets (small windows within the Tk window) for input and display structures. Ruby has its own interface, RMagick, to the ImageMagick image manipulation language.

If you install ImageMagick, RMagick, and Tk onto your computer, you can "require" them into your Ruby scripts and create applications that create, modify, evaluate, and display images. All three applications are available at no cost for users of Windows or UNIX/Linux operating systems. Ample instruction is available at the websites listed next.

Here are some instructions for Windows users who may want to try these extensions:

1. Go to the RubyForge site and download the combined RMagick and ImageMagick binaries. The URL for RubyForge is

   `http://rubyforge.org/frs/?group_id=12&release_id=8170`

   This page has a combined win32 binary package for RMagick and ImageMagick. Pick the binary that is appropriate for your computer's version of Ruby.

2. Download the binary (zip file) and expand it. This produces a number of files, one of which is the ImageMagick `.exe` file.

3. Run the ImageMagick `.exe` file, and it will guide you through its installation.

4. After ImageMagick is installed, you can install the RMagick RubyGem by invoking Ruby's `gem` tool with an `install` command followed by the file name (add the full path to the `gem` file if you are not installing from its current subdirectory). For example,

   `c:\>gem install rmagick-1.13.0-win32.gem`

5. All of the information you need to start using RMagick from within your own Ruby Scripts is found at

   `http://www.simplesystems.org/RMagick/doc/`

6. Install Tcl/Tk. A popular version of Tcl/Tk can be obtained by visiting ActiveState (`http://www.activestate.com`) and downloading the binary for Windows users.

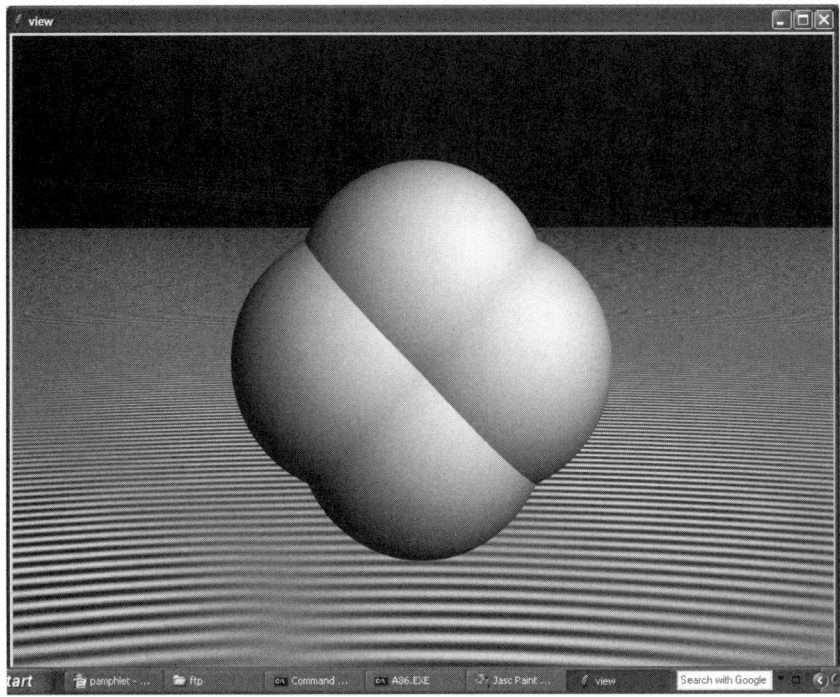

Figure 2 *Outputting an image using ImageMagick, Tk, and RMagick. The image is shown in its Tk widget (labeled "view") within the computer monitor's desktop display.*

Now you are ready to write Ruby scripts that use and display images. You can load a `jpeg` file with RMagick and display it in a window with Tk. An example is shown here. The image, `uni4_bw.jpg` is converted into a `gif` image and displayed in a Tk widget on your computer's desktop (Figure 2).

```ruby
#!/usr/local/bin/ruby
require 'RMagick'
include Magick
leaf = ImageList.new("uni4_bw.jpg").resize!(0.7)
leaf_copy = leaf.write("uni4_bw.gif")
require 'tk'
root = TkRoot.new {title "view"}
TkButton.new(root) do
  image TkPhotoImage.new{file "uni4_bw.gif"}
  command {exit}
  pack
end
Tk.mainloop
exit
```

Modules

A Ruby module is a section of invoked code that contains methods and constants assigned to a namespace (the declared module name). A module can be included in the class definition of several unrelated classes, which in turn allows these unrelated classes to access some of the same module methods. In Ruby jargon, modules distributed within classes are called "Mixins."

Modules are the heart of compositional object programming, wherein classes acquire nonhierarchical methods that enhance the functionality of the class without changing the identity and the purpose of the class. Many of the built-in Ruby classes contain modules that are common to other Ruby classes. One of the most important differences between modules and classes is that modules do not create object instances of themselves.

Modules are one example of advanced object-oriented methods that cannot be covered in depth in this short introduction to Ruby.

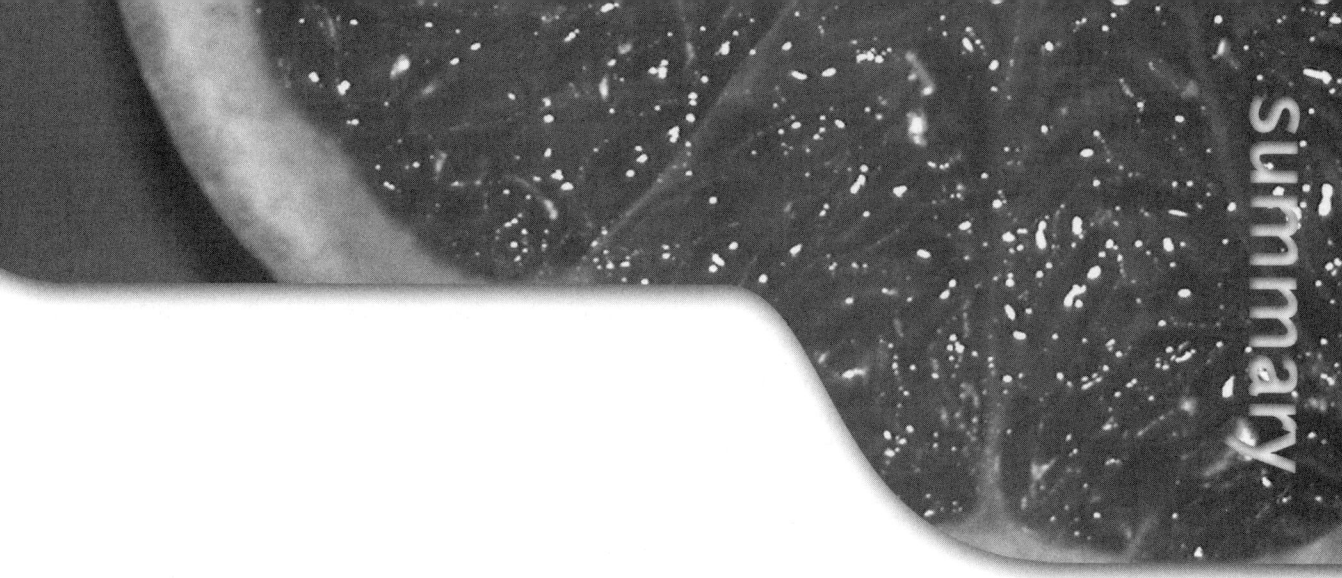

Ruby is an example of a pure object-oriented programming language. Everything within the language (data, constants, code blocks, methods) is an object, and the language achieves its functionality by sending methods to objects. The rapid growth in Ruby's popularity has resulted from its many useful features—none unique to Ruby—that converge to produce one of the best programming languages in existence.

1. Ruby is easy to learn. Nonprogrammers can write simple Ruby programs after only a few hours of instruction.

2. Ruby is a freely available, no-cost, open-source language.

3. Ruby is available for many different operating systems, and a script written for one operating system will work when run from the command line of another operating system.

4. Ruby has worldwide popularity. A large and enthusiastic community of Ruby programmers is constantly enhancing the Ruby language and increasing the number of available class libraries and Ruby extensions.

5. Ruby is a scripting language. It does not require a special programming environment, and the scripts can be transported as simple, pure text files.

6. Ruby's syntax is similar to the syntax of both Perl and Python. Ruby contains built-in methods that replicate most of the functionality that Perl and Python programmers have come to expect. Ruby scripts can be understood by most programmers who use these languages, and Perl and Python programmers can easily transition their skills into Ruby.

7. Ruby enforces one-class ancestry: A method called and sent from Ruby will have a class source that is completely predetermined. In languages that support multiple-class inheritance, the method received by an object may not always be predetermined, which can lead to unstable programs. In Ruby, classes can be modified to include methods found in other classes through the use of modules, a logical and safe way to realize some of the useful features of multiple-class inheritance.

8. In Ruby, statements can be evaluated as true, false, or `nil`. Most languages (Perl included) are restricted to a true/false dichotomy and do not evaluate statements that are neither true nor false. Ruby's `NilClass` class supports logical constructions that would be impossible or difficult to achieve in many other languages.

9. Ruby permits method chaining, allowing highly complex calculations to be written concisely in a single line of code. Chaining, along with other high-level runtime evaluation operations (such as code block evaluation and closures), is easily accomplished in Ruby.

10. Ruby has built-in Regex (regular expressions) support. Regex is a string pattern-matching shorthand that is shared among many different languages (Perl and Python) and meta-languages (XML). Languages that lack Regex cannot easily be used in programs that parse files for string patterns—an increasingly important computational task encountered in many different scientific fields.

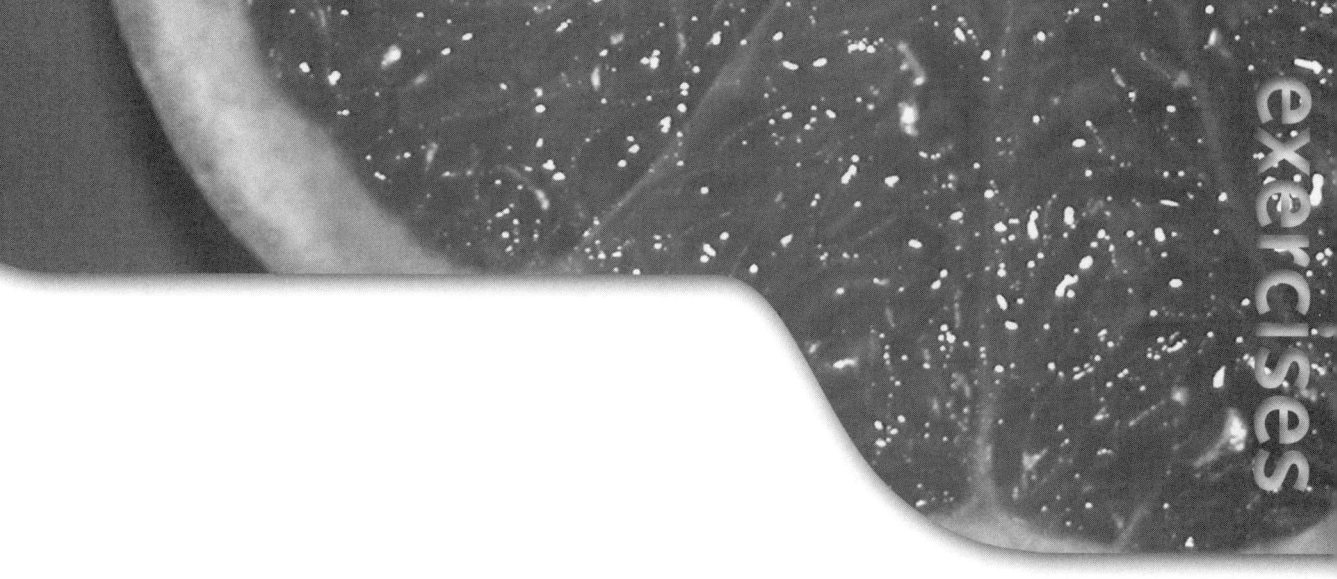

1. What is an object-oriented programming language?

2. What is the Ruby `irb` environment?

3. What is the difference between a class object and an instance object?

4. What is a class hierarchy?

5. What is the fundamental syntax of a Ruby statement?

6. What is method polymorphism?

7. Write a script that adds the numbers in a list and determines the mean.

8. Write a script that parses a text file, extracts the words that occur one or more times in the file, and creates an alphabetized list of the words.

9. Write a script that parses a text file and determines the frequencies (number of occurrences) of each word in the file.

10. Write a script that parses a text file and determine the byte locations of each word in the file.

11. Write a script that prompts a user for a search word and produces the byte locations in a text file where the search word occurs.

12. Write a script that prompts a user for a search phrase (more than one word) and produces the byte locations in a text file where the phrase occurs.

13. Write a script that prompts a user for a search phrase and then lists all of the sentences in a text file that contains the phrase.

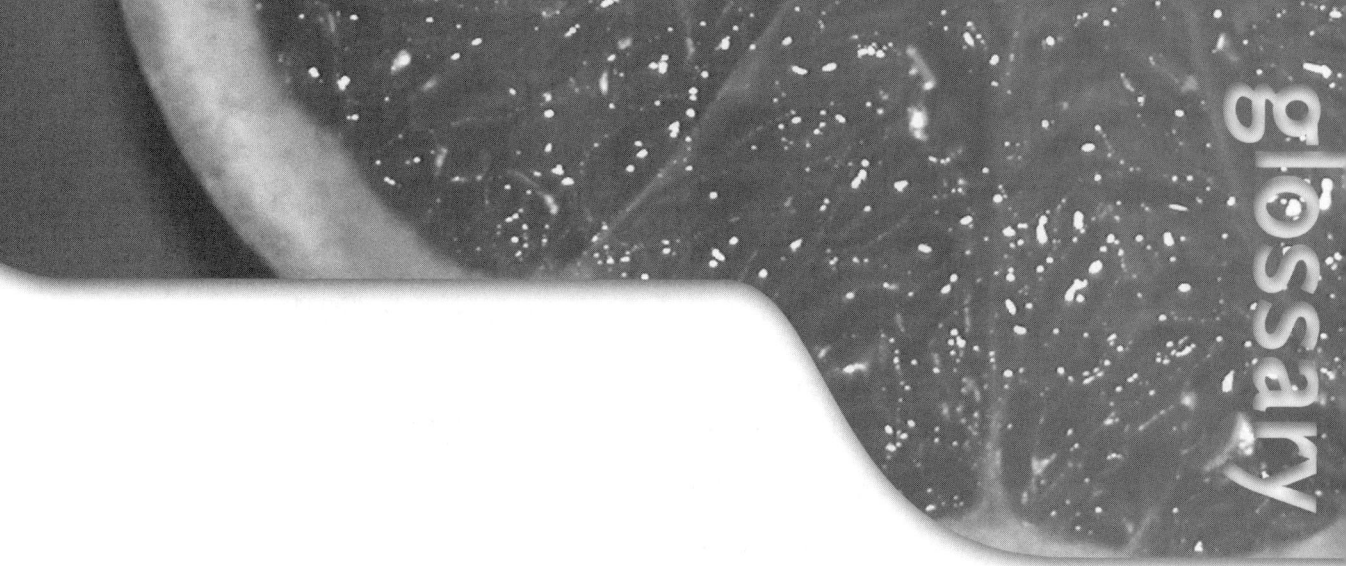

close (IO#close)   Closes an IO object (usually a file) and returns nil. After an IO object is closed, it is unavailable for read or write operations (until reopened).

```
irb>text = File.open("ruby.txt", "r") => #<File:ruby.txt>
irb>text.close => nil
```

collect (Enumerable#collect)   Ruby has built-in iterators (each, find, collect, inject) that invoke a block of code for each of the elements of an object and returns an array consisting of the evaluated result of each iteration.

```
irb>[1,2,3,4,5].collect{|element| element=0 unless element>3}=>
[0, 0, 0, nil, nil]
```

each (IO#each)   The class IO each iterator parses a file of any size one line at a time. An example is shown here with some pseudocode:

```
corpus_file = File.open("pubmed.txt")
corpus_file.each do
|line|
<something here>
<something here>
end
```

find (Enumerable#find)   Ruby has built-in iterators (each, find, collect, inject) that invoke a block of code for each of the elements of an object and return some output determined by the iterator. The find iterator yields the first iterated element that yields a true value for an expression contained in the block. For example,

```
irb>[1,2,3,4,5].find{|x| x > 4} => 5
irb>[1,2,3,4,5,6].find{|x| x > 4} => 5
```

first (Array#first)   This method operates on instance objects of class `Array` and returns the zeroth element of the array.

```
irb>myarray = %w[6 9 4 100] => ["6", "9", "4", "100"]
irb>myarray.first => "6"
```

foreach (Dir#foreach)   This iterator method appears in several classes. In the `Dir` class, `foreach` is a class method that calls a block for each file name in a directory. For example,

```
Dir.foreach("."){|file| puts(file)}
```

prints the files in the current directory, one file name per line.

foreach (IO#foreach)   This iterator method appears in several classes. In the `IO` class, `foreach` executes a block for every iterated line in the `IO` object (usually a file).

gets (IO#gets)   The class `IO` `gets` method reads the next line from the designated IO stream. When the IO stream is `STDIN` (standard input device, or keyboard), Ruby collects the keyboarded input and assigns it to a string object. The last character key entered is the Enter key, which sends a newline character to the input. It is customary to remove the newline character from the input line with class `String`'s `chomp!` method. The `chomp!` method removes the newline character (or any designated line separator) if it is present at the end of a line, and returns the shortened line.

```
#!/usr/bin/ruby
puts "Enter anything and press the Enter key"
input = STDIN.gets.chomp!
puts "You just entered \"#{input}\""
exit
```

Output and interaction:

```
C:\>ruby get.rb
Enter anything and press the Enter key
hello world
You just entered "hello world"
```

glob (Dir#glob)   Ruby's own version of the venerable UNIX `glob` command collects files through a wildcard filter. The example creates a list of all files in the current directory.

```
#!/usr/local/bin/ruby
print((Dir.glob("*")).join("\n"))
exit
```

gsub (String#gsub)   This method substitutes a substring within a string at every location where a matching pattern is found. The `sub` method works like `gsub` but makes only one substitution at the first match. For example,

```
irb>"Rabies is great".sub(/a/,'u').gsub(/ies/,'y')
=> "Ruby is great"
```

inject (Enumerable#inject)   Ruby has built-in iterators (each, find, collect, inject) that invoke a block of code for each of the elements of an object and return some output determined by the iterator. The inject iterator accrues a value across all the members of a collection. For example,

```
irb>[-1,0,1,2,3].inject(0) {|total, x| total + x} => 5
```

The inject method operates over ranges as well as arrays:

```
irb>(1..30).inject(0){|accum,x|accum + x} => 465
```

instance_methods (Module#instance_methods)   This method returns an array listing the public instance methods available to a module or class. The methods of class Module are available to all Ruby modules and classes. The following statement collects the instance methods that belong to class Fixnum but that do not belong to its ancestor class, Numeric:

```
irb>(Fixnum.instance_methods - Numeric.instance_methods).join(" ")
=>
"% to_r << rdiv > prec_f & size to_bn * next +
gcd rpower - id2name / denominator | ~ downto to_sym ^ lcm
upto prec ** power! times numerator succ to_i gcdlcm prec_i
chr [] to_f"
```

join (Array#join)   In the Array class, join concatenates each element of an array, separated by the provided parameter. For example,

```
#!/usr/local/bin/ruby
print((Dir.glob("*")).join("\n"))
exit
```

The output would consist of a list of all files and subdirectories in the current directory, with each element of the list separated by a newline character.

keys (Hash#keys)   This method returns the array of keys in a Hash object. For example,

```
#!/usr/local/bin/ruby
freq = Hash.new(0)
my_string = "A man, a plan, a canal, Panama"
my_string.downcase.scan(/\w+/){|word| freq[word] = freq[word]+1}
freq.keys.sort.each {|k| print k, " - ", freq[k], "\n"}
exit
```

new   The most important purpose of a class is to create class instances. This is done through the `new` method. Some classes have their own `new` method; other classes have no `new` method of their own and depend on the existence of an ancestral `new`. Examples are as follows:

```
some_array = Array.new
some_hash = Hash.new
```

open (IO#open)   The class IO open method prepares an IO object (usually a file) for reading or writing. If the file does not exist, it calls the `new` method and creates a file.

```
text = File.open("anatomy.txt", "r")
```

Opens file `anatomy.txt` for reading.

```
outf = File.open("objects.txt", "w")
```

Opens file `objects.txt` for writing (accepting input).

print (IO#print)   This method prints objects. For example,

```
out.print(value, "\n")
```

prints to the `out` object (usually a file object).

```
my_hash.each {|key,value| STDOUT.print(key, " --- ", value, "\n")}
```

For each key/value pair in the hash, this statement prints to the computer monitor the key followed by a space, three hyphens, and another space, followed by the value followed by the newline character.

puts (Kernel#puts)   This useful alternative to `print` automatically adds a newline character to an object and prints to the standard output by default.

rand (Kernel#rand)   This method returns a pseudo-random floating-point number between 0 and a provided integer or between 0 and 1 if 0 is provided as an argument. For example,

```
irb>rand(0) => 0.432647535748461
```

read (IO#read class method)   This method enters an IO object (usually a file) and returns a string of a provided length beginning from a provided offset byte in the file. Without length and offset parameters, `read` will return the entire file as a string. Here is its syntax:

```
read(filename,length_of_string,file_offset)
```

Th next example prints file named `anatomy.rb` to the computer screen:

```
irb> print(IO.read("anatomy.rb"))
```

require (Kernel#require)   When the Ruby interpreter encounters a require statement followed by the name of an external Ruby file (you can omit the .rb extension from the file name), it pulls in and evaluates the external code. Ruby will raise a LoadError exception if it cannot find the required file.

seek (IO#seek)   Every good programming language contains operators that allow program-mers to access any desired byte location within a file (random access to files). In Ruby, the seek method moves to a particular byte location in a file or IO object. The byte location is determined by a starting position in the file, offset by a preferred number of bytes. The syntax is as follows:

```
fileobject.seek(offset,from_location)
```

The offset is an integer that should not exceed the number of bytes in the file. There are three allowed values for from_location:

```
IO::SEEK_CUR
```

Begins from the current reading location in the file.

```
IO::SEEK_END
```

Begins from the end of the file and expects a negative number for the offset to indicate the number of bytes from the end of the file.

```
IO::SEEK_SET
```

Begins from the beginning byte in the file.

shift (Array#shift)   This method finds the first element of an array (element number zero) and removes it from the array. For example,

```
irb> my_array = [1,2,3] => [1, 2, 3]
irb> my_array.shift => 1
irb> my_array => [2, 3]
```

size (Array#size)   This method returns the number of elements in an array. For example,

```
irb> ["l","e","y","l","b"].size => 5
```

slice (Array#slice)   This method returns a subset of an array. For example,

```
irb>["l","e","y","l","b"].slice(0..2) => ["l", "e", "y"]
```

sort (Array#sort)   This method sorts an array in alphabetic order. For example,

```
irb>["l","e","y","l","b"].sort.join => "belly"
```

split (String#split)   Class String's split method is used in virtually every script that parses strings of words. The split method breaks a string at locations in the string that match a provided pattern and returns an array. The syntax is shown here:

```
my_string.split(regexpattern, number_of_returned_elements).
```

If no pattern is provided, split divides a string on the space character. If the number of returned elements is not provided, split matches every pattern in the string. Some examples follow:

```
irb>my_string = String.new("calcifying epithelioma of Malherbe")
=> "calcifying epithelioma of Malherbe"
irb>my_string.split
=> ["calcifying", "epithelioma", "of", "Malherbe"]
irb>my_string.split(/e/)
=> ["calcifying ", "pith", "lioma of Malh", "rb"]
irb>my_string.split(/e/,2)
=> ["calcifying ", "pithelioma of Malherbe"]
irb>my_string.split(//)
=> ["c", "a", "l", "c", "i", "f", "y", "i", "n", "g", " ",
"e", "p", "i", "t", "h", "e", "l", "i", "o", "m", "a", " ",
"o", "f", " ", "M", "a", "l", "h", "e", "r", "b", "e"]
```

super (Object#super)   This method calls the parent class's version of the method of the same name as the calling method's name. The super method provides a way to access methods of a parent class that may have been overridden in the child class.

```
class Person < String
def downcase
  puts "Calling Person's superclass method"
  super #calls String class's downcase method
end
end
```

superclass (Class#superclass)   Ruby contains many reflection methods, which are designed to provide information about the role of the object in the Ruby object hierarchy. One such method is superclass, a method of class Class, that returns the name of the ancestor class.

```
irb>Array.superclass => Object
irb>Hash.superclass => Object
irb>Object.superclass => nil
irb>Class.superclass => Module
```

to_f (Fixnum#to_f)   Ruby has several subclasses under class Numeric, including Bignum, Fixnum, and Float. All of these classes have a to_f method that will convert objects in their class to a float that can be used in the high-precision mathematical methods included in class Float.

```
irb> my_number = 4  => 4
irb> my_number.to_f => 4.0
```

unshift (Array#unshift)   This method does the opposite of shift: It adds an element to the front of an array.

```
irb> my_array = [1,2,3] => [1, 2, 3]
irb> my_array.unshift("apple") => ["apple", 1, 2, 3]
```

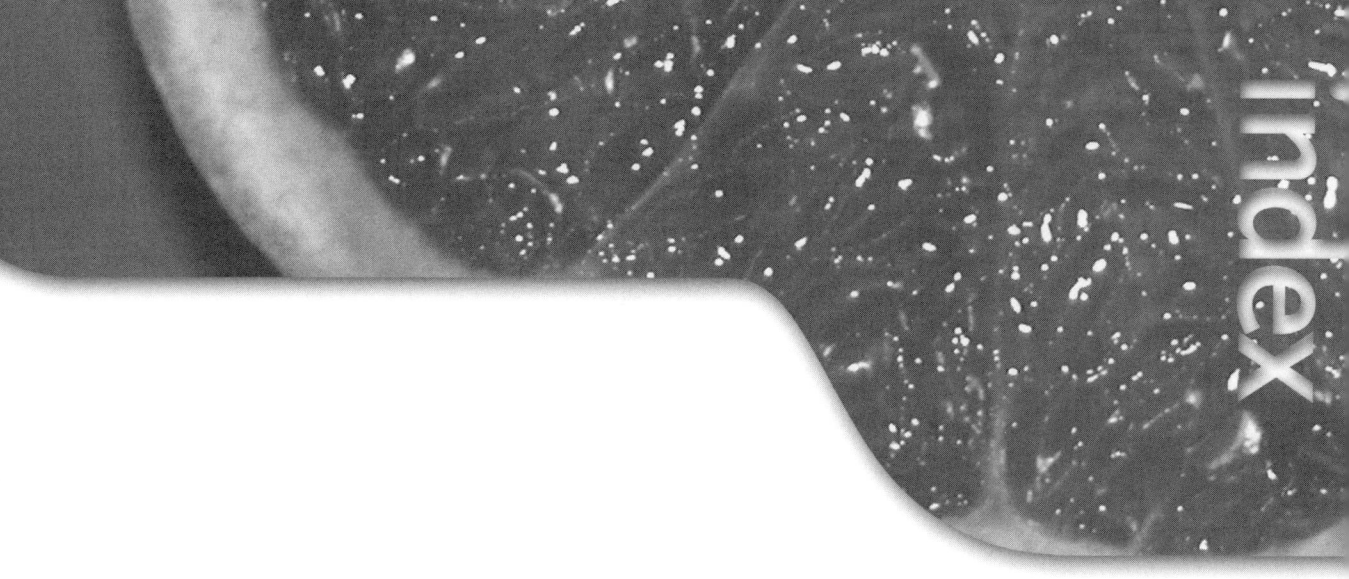